CASSANDRA L. WILLIAMS

Be Not Deceived

Unmasking the Cycle

YAH
Publishing

TABLE OF CONTENTS

Acknowledgments

Acknowledgment of Love and Gratitude

To my amazing sons, Elijah, Jeremiah and Isaiah and my precious granddaughter, Audrey.

Your love, strength and unwavering presence have been my anchor through some of the toughest moments in my life. Each of you has brought light, purpose and joy into my world in your own unique way.

Elijah, your wisdom and resilience inspire me every day. **Jeremiah**, your kindness and steady spirit have brought comfort in my hardest moments. **Isaiah**, your courage and heart remind me to keep pushing forward no matter what. **Audrey**, your sweet smile and pure innocence fill my heart with endless love and hope.

I am incredibly proud of each of you, and I thank God for the gift of having you in my life. No matter where life takes us, my love for you will remain constant and strong.

I love you always, beyond words, beyond time and beyond measure.

"Break the Silence"

"I was taught to shrink, to fade and hide,

To bury my truth deep inside.

I was told that silence was safer than screams,

And bruises would fade like forgotten dreams.

But pain has memory, and wounds still speak,

Even when voices are trembling and weak.

A fist, a word, and a cruel embrace

Left scars too deep for time to erase.

No more chains, and no more fear!

I break the cycle I make it clear.

My voice is fire, my soul is free,

I rise, I roar, and I choose me.

I choose to break the silence.

And stand for the weak.

Give voice to the voiceless, and to all who've been told not to speak."

Written by: Cassandra L. Williams

CHAPTER 1

BREAKING THE SILENCE

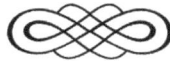

The Hidden Struggles:

The hidden struggles are the most dangerous secrets that remain unspoken. For countless young people, the silence surrounding domestic violence and unhealthy relationships becomes an invisible cage, locking them away from the support they need. It's a silence filled with shame, fear and confusion. A silence that grows louder with every moment unaddressed. But breaking that silence is the first step toward freedom.

Domestic violence isn't just something that happens behind closed doors in homes. It's happening everywhere, at school, on social media and even in friendships and young relationships. According to studies, 1 in 3 teenagers in the United States experiences some form of dating abuse before they turn 18 years old. Yet, despite its prevalence, many young people don't even realize they are caught in a harmful cycle.

This book is for you… the young person who may be wondering if what you're experiencing is normal? It's for the friend who has seen red flags but doesn't know how to intervene? It's for the parent, teacher or mentor who wants to help but doesn't know where to start? It's for anyone ready to break the silence and begin the journey toward healing and empowerment.

Why, we stay silent:

Silence often feels like the safest option. For many, speaking up about abuse seems like opening Pandora's box, a chaotic mess that can't be contained. But silence comes at a cost. It allows fear to thrive and keeps those who are suffering isolated.

There are many reasons young people stay silent about abuse:

1. Fear of judgment: "What will people think of me?"

2. Confusion: "Is this really abuse, or am I overreacting?"

3. Loyalty: "I don't want to hurt or betray someone I care about."

4. Shame: "This is my fault… I should've seen it coming."

5. Lack of Awareness: "I didn't know there was another way?"

Karen's Story: A Life in the Shadows

Fifteen-year-old, Karen seemed to have it all together. She excelled in school she was the captain of her soccer team and always had a smile on her face for her friends. But at home, life was a different story. Her stepfather's temper controlled every aspect of their household. What started as small criticisms such as, "You're not smart enough", or "You'll never mount to anything", quickly escalated to shouting matches, broken dishes and doors slammed so hard they shook the walls.

Karen didn't tell anyone. She convinced herself that it wasn't all that bad. Because the stepfather didn't hit her. But the constant verbal attacks left her feeling worthless. Her mental health started spiraling down, she became withdrawn from her friends, and she stopped trying in school. She believed the lies that her stepfather said about her. Until one day, Karen was introduced to art therapy. Karen joined an art therapy program at the local community center, and she began to see her situation for what it was, abuse. For the first time, she found a safe place to express what she was feeling.

Through painting, she began to process her pain, and through the support of her peers and mentors, she found her voice. Breaking her silence was the hardest thing she had ever done, but it was the most freeing feeling ever.

Why Breaking the Silence Matters

Karen's story highlights an important truth. Speaking up can be terrifying, but it's also the first step toward change.

When we speak up, we:

♦ Acknowledge the Problem: Naming the issue is a powerful way to take control of it.

♦ Find Support: Silence isolates but speaking out builds connection.

♦ Empower Others: Every time one person shares their story, it creates a ripple effect of courage.

Breaking the silence doesn't always mean making a public announcement. It can be as simple as telling a trusted friend, counselor, or a teacher. The important thing is to start somewhere.

The Ripple Effect of Speaking Out

When one person finds the courage to speak up, they inspire others to do the same. Consider the story of Andre, a spoken word artist who turned his pain into poetry. As a child, Andre witnessed his father verbally and physically abuse his mother. For years, he bottled up his feelings, afraid of what others would think if they knew? But in high school, he discovered spoken word and began performing pieces about his experience. His words resonated with others, sparking conversations and encouraging peers to share their stories. What started as a personal outlet became a powerful platform for change.

What Breaking the Silence Looks Like

Breaking the silence doesn't look the same for everyone. Here are a few ways to start:

1. Talk to Someone You Trust: Whether it's a friend, family member, teacher, or counselor, find someone who will listen without judgment.

2. Express Yourself Creatively: Write a poem, draw a picture, or write in a journal.

3. Sometimes, the act of creating can help clarify your thoughts and emotions.

4. Educate Yourself: Learn about the signs of abuse and the resources available to help.

5. Knowledge is power.

6. Join a Support Group: Surround yourself with others who understand what you're going through.

A Journey, not a Destination

Breaking the silence is just the beginning. It's the first step on a journey toward healing, self-discovery, and empowerment. It won't always be easy, and there will be setbacks along the way. But every step forward... no matter how small, is a victory.

In the chapters ahead, we'll dive deeper into the cycle of violence, explore the red flags to watch for, and discover how creativity and community can help us heal. Together, we'll uncover the tools to not just survive but thrive. Remember, you are not alone, and your story matters.

"Cycle of Violence"

"It starts with a whisper, a wound left unseen.

A pain that lingers where love should have been.

Passed down like echoes stained with cries,

Unspoken lessons, in a home built on lies.

One hand lifts another recoil now trembles of fear,

A voice that was hopeful fades year after year.

A child learns the rhythm of anger and shame,

Taught that survival is playing the game.

Yet, somewhere within, a seed starts to grow.

A whisper of healing, a truth they must know.

That chains can be broken, and the cycle can end.

Pain can be rewritten, and hearts can transcend."

Written By: Cassandra L. Williams

CHAPTER 2

THE CYCLE OF VIOLENCE

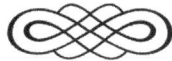

Patterns that Trap Us

Abuse doesn't start with bruises or broken glass... it begins with subtle patterns that are easy to miss. Many people think domestic violence is only physical, but it often starts long before a single hand is raised. As its core, abuse is about control, and understanding the Cycle of Violence is key to recognizing how abuse takes root and why it can feel impossible to escape.

This chapter will break down the stages of the cycle, provide real-life examples, and help you understand the psychological traps that keep people stuck. When you learn to spot these patterns, you take the first step toward breaking free.

The Cycle of Violence

The Cycle of Violence is a repeating pattern of behavior that often defines abusive relationships. It has four key phrases:

1. The Honeymoon Phase
2. The Tension-Building Phase

3. The Explosion

4. The Calm

Each phase serves a purpose for the abuser, making it harder for the victim to leave. Let's dive into each stage.

1. The Honeymoon Phase: When Everything Feels Perfect

At the start of a relationship, or after an abusive incident, the abuser often seems loving, attentive, and apologetic. They might shower the victim with gifts, affection, and promises to change. This phase is designed to rebuild trust and convince the victim that the abuse was an isolated incident.

Scenario

Maria started dating her boyfriend, Alex, when she was 16. At first, he was charming and thoughtful and always asking her how her day was going? He often surprised her with flowers and talked about their future together. After a big argument where Alex yelled and called her names, he apologized profusely. He promised it would never happen again, writing her a long, heartfelt letter. Maria forgave him, believing he meant it.

Why it's Dangerous:

The Honeymoon Phase creates confusion. Victims often think, "This is the real person they are... the kind, loving version." They convince themselves the abuse was a mistake, not a pattern. This makes it harder to recognize the behavior as abuse.

2. The Tension-Building Phase: Walking on Eggshells

As time passes, tension begins to build. The abuser becomes more irritable, critical or controlling. Small disagreements can feel like ticking time bombs, leaving the victim anxious and on the edge.

Scenario

Alex started complaining when Maria wanted to spend time with her friends. "Why do you need them when you have me?" he would say. He began texting her constantly, accusing her of ignoring him if she didn't respond right away. Maria felt like she had to be extra careful not to upset him.

Why It's Dangerous:

During this phase, the victim might try to modify their behavior to avoid triggering the abuser. They may start blaming them- selves, thinking, "if I just try harder, I can keep them happy." This self-blame deepens the victim's feelings of isolation and helplessness.

3. The Explosion: When the Abuse Happens

This is the phase most people associate with domestic violence. It's the point when the tension reaches a breaking point, and the abuser lashes out physically, emotionally and verbally. The abuse may take the form of yelling, hitting, threats or manipulation.

Scenario

One night, Alex became furious when Maria didn't text him back within ten minutes. He called her repeatedly, leaving angry voicemails. When she answered, he yelled at her, accusing her of cheating and saying she didn't care about him. The next day at school, he refused to speak to her, leaving Maria in tears.

Why It's Dangerous:

The Explosion phase is where the abuse is most obvious. And it's also the point where victims feel the most powerless.

They may feel frozen, unsure how to respond or where to turn for help.

4. The Calm: The False Normal

After the explosion, the abuser may enter the Calm phase, acting as if nothing happened. They might ignore the incident entirely or downplay its significance, making the victim question their own experience. This phase often overlaps with the Honeymoon phase, as the abuser seeks to re-establish control through apologies or affection.

Scenario

After ignoring Maria for days, Alex finally texted her, saying, "I overreacted. I'm so sorry. I just love you so much, and I get scared of losing you." He promised to do better and convinced Maria to stay in the relationship.

Why It's Dangerous:

The Calm phase can be deeply confusing. Victims may convince themselves that the worst is over and that things will improve, only for the cycle to repeat.

How the Cycle Feeds Itself

Each phase of the Cycle of Violence reinforces the abuser's control and deepens the victim's dependence. Here's how:

- ◆ **The Honeymoon Phase:** Gives the victim hope that the relationship will improve.

- ◆ **The Tension-Building Phase:** Trains the victim to accept blame and modify their behavior.

- ◆ **The Explosion:** Instills fear, making the victim feel powerless to leave.

- ◆ **The Calm:** Creates confusion and reinforces the abuser's control.

Why the Cycle is So Hard to Break

- **Emotional Manipulation:** Abusers often use guilt, love, or fear to keep their victims in the relationship.

- **Isolation:** Victims may feel cut off from friends, family or resources, making them feel like they have nowhere to turn.

- **Self-Blame:** Many victims believe the abuse is their fault and that they must fix the relationship.

- **Hope:** The Honeymoon phase convinces victims that change is possible, keeping them trapped in the cycle.

Breaking the Cycle

Breaking free from the Cycle of Violence requires courage, support, and a plan. Here are some steps to start:

- **Recognize the Pattern:** Awareness is the first step. Acknowledge the cycle and how it affects you.

- **Reach Out:** Talk to someone you trust such as a friend, counselor, family or hotline. You don't have to do this alone.

- **Make a Safety Plan:** If you're in immediate danger, have a plan for where to go and how to get help.

- **Seek Professional Help:** Therapists and support groups can provide tools and guidance for healing.

Conclusion: Understanding is Power

The Cycle of Violence thrives on silence and confusion. But understanding its patterns gives you the power to break free. Whether you're experiencing abuse yourself or supporting someone who is, knowing how the cycle works is a vital first step.

In the next chapter, we'll dive deeper into how to recognize red flags early. So, you can protect yourself and others.

"Red Flags"

"Their words are like gold,

But listen close because some truths aren't told.

A charm too thick, and a pace too fast,

A love that burns but doesn't last.

They dodge the questions, and shift the blame

Make you feel crazy and feed you shame.

Apologies like empty air,

Yet when you need them, they're not there.

Your gut is screaming, Yet, you stay,

Ignoring signs along the way.

But red flags wave for those who see,

A warning call: "Come set yourself free!" Respect should never come with chains,

Love should never bring you pain.

So, trust the signs, don't play their game,

Know your worth and protect your flame.

When red flags rise, don't hesitate,

Walk away before it's to late."

Written By: Cassandra L. Williams

CHAPTER 3

RECOGNIZING RED FLAGS

∞

The Warning Signs We Ignore

R ed flags don't always look like bright neon signs. They often start as subtle shifts, small uneasy feelings that we push aside, thinking, maybe I'm overreacting. But ignoring the signs of an unhealthy relationship can lead to emotional harm, manipulation, and even physical danger.

Understanding red flags is crucial because abuse doesn't happen all at once. It's a gradual process, starting with small controlling behaviors before escalating into more serious harm. **In this chapter, we'll explore the most common red flags in relationships, friendships, and family dynamics. So, you can recognize the warning signs before it's too late.**

1. The Red Flags of an Unhealthy Relationship

Romantic relationships should be built on **trust, respect and support...** not on control, fear or manipulation. Here are some common red flags that signal an unhealthy relationship:

A. Controlling Behavior

♦ Your partner tells you who you can and can't hang out with.

♦ They constantly check your phone or social media without permission.

♦ They make decisions for you, from what you wear to where you go.

Scenario

Taylor, 16, was excited to wear a new dress to school, but her boyfriend, Jordan, told her it was "too revealing" and that she should change. At first, she thought he was just being protective, but soon he started telling her what to wear every day. When she tried to resist, he accused her of disrespecting him.

Why It's Dangerous:

Control is not love. A healthy relationship allows both people to make choices freely.

B. Jealousy Disguised as Love

♦ Your partner constantly accuses you of flirting or cheating.

♦ They get upset if you spend time with family or friends.

♦ They say, "I just love you so much, I can't stand to see you with anyone else."

Scenario

Derek started dating his girlfriend, Maya, freshman year. At first, he was sweet and affectionate, but soon, he began questioning her about every guy she talked to. If she didn't text back quickly enough, he assumed she was cheating. He told her, "If you really love me, you'll prove it by not talking to any other guys." Maya felt trapped and she didn't want to lose him. But she also felt like she was losing herself.

Why It's Dangerous:

Jealousy may seem like a sign of love, but it is a sign of insecurity and control.

C. Blaming You for Their Actions

◆ They say, "If you didn't make me mad, I wouldn't have yelled at you."

◆ They twist situations to make you feel guilty for their behavior.

◆ They never take responsibility for their actions.

Why It's Dangerous:

If someone refuses to take responsibility for their actions, the behavior will continue. You are not responsible for someone else's toxic choices.

D. Walking On Eggshells

◆ You feel nervous about expressing your feelings because you don't want to upset them.

◆ You constantly adjust your behavior to avoid setting them off.

◆ You feel like you're in a relationship with two different people... one loving and one scary.

Scenario

Every time Lisa and her boyfriend, Chris, fought, he would ignore her for days. She found herself apologizing for things she didn't even do, just to make him happy again. Over time, she stopped bringing up things that upset her because she feared how he would react.

Why It's Dangerous:

Love should not be based on fear. If you're afraid of someone's reaction, the relationship is unhealthy.

2. The Red Flags in Friendships

Toxic friendships can be just as damaging as toxic romantic relationships. Here are some signs of unhealthy friendships:

A. They Constantly Put You Down

+ They make fun of you but say, "I'm just joking."

+ They embarrass you in front of others to make themselves look better.

+ They dismiss your feelings when you express hurt.

Why It's Dangerous:

True friends build you up, not tear you down.

B. They Only Call You When They Need Something

+ They disappear when you need them but expect you to be there for them.

+ They never celebrate your successes or check on you unless they need a favor.

Why It's Dangerous:

Friendship should be mutual, not one-sided.

C. They Use Guilt to Control You

+ They say, "If you don't do this, you're a bad friend."

+ They make you feel responsible for their happiness.

Why It's Dangerous:
Friendships should be about respect, not obligation.

3. The Red Flags in Family Relationships
Not all unhealthy relationships are romantic. Sometimes, family members can be emotionally or physically abusive.

A. They Disrespect Your Boundaries
◆ They invade your personal space without permission.

◆ They demand control over your life, even when you're old enough to make your own choices.

Why It's Dangerous:
Boundaries are important in every relationship, even within families.

B. They Use Fear and Threats
◆ They make you feel like you have to obey them or face serious consequences.

◆ They use phrases like, "If you don't do what I say, you'll regret it."

Why It's Dangerous:
Fear should never be the foundation of a relationship.

4. How to Protect Yourself
Now that you know the red flags, what can you do about them? Here are some steps to protect yourself:

A. Trust Your Gut
If something feels off, it probably is. Your instincts are powerful.

B. Set Clear Boundaries

Say no to toxic behavior and stick to it.

C. Seek Support

Talk to a friend, teacher, counselor, or trusted adult about what's happening.

D. Plan Your Exit

If you're in a dangerous situation, have a plan for how to leave safely.

1. Recognizing the Difference Between Love and Control A healthy relationship includes:

♦ Mutual Respect

♦ Open Communication

♦ Freedom to Be Yourself

An unhealthy relationship includes:

♦ **Control and Jealousy**

♦ **Blame and Manipulation**

♦ **Fear and Isolation**

1. The Power of Walking

Leaving a toxic situation is not a sign of weakness. It's a sign of strength. Whether it's a toxic friendship, a harmful family dynamic or an abusive relationship, you have the right to protect your peace.

Jasmine's Story:

Jasmine, 17, was in an emotionally abusive relationship for two years. Her boyfriend constantly criticized her, controlled what she wore, and guilt-tripped her into staying. When she finally left, she felt lost at first. But over some time, she rediscovered her confidence. Today, she speaks at youth events about recognizing red flags, using her experience to help others.

Conclusion: You Deserve Better

You are worthy of relationships built on love, trust and respect. Recognizing red flags is the first step to protecting yourself from harm. If you see warning signs in your relationship, take them seriously.

The next chapter will explore the power of healing through creativity, how music, spoken word and art can help process pain and find strength.

Remember, If, you or someone you know is in danger, reach out to a trusted adult, counselor or a support hotline.

"Power of the Healing Arts"

"There is a power, soft yet strong,
Where pain transforms into a song.
A canvas stretched, and a voice set free,
A space where hearts can truly breathe.
The dancers move and the poets speak,
The rhythm lifts where words can't reach.
A sculpted piece or a melody
Turns aching hearts to moving feet.
The healing arts are both fierce and kind.
Arts unchain the soul and renew the mind.
We find a pulse of our beating heart
Through the power of the healing arts."
Written By: Cassandra L. Williams

CHAPTER 4

HEALING THROUGH THE ARTS

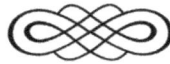

The Power of Creativity in Healing

Pain can be difficult to put into words. Sometimes, the weight of trauma feels too heavy to speak aloud, and emotions remain locked inside, waiting for release. But healing doesn't always come through talking, it can come through creating.

Art has long been used as a tool for healing. Whether it's through spoken word, music, painting, dance or storytelling, creative expression allows people to process emotions, regain control over their narrative, and find peace.

This chapter explores how the healing arts can be used to recover from trauma, reconnect with oneself, and build resilience.

1. Why the Arts Are a Powerful Healing Tool

Healing from trauma, especially the effects of domestic violence, emotional abuse and toxic relationships, isn't just about moving on; it's about rebuilding **self-worth, confidence and emotional stability.** The arts can help because they:

- ◆ Provide a safe way to express emotions without judgment.

- ◆ Help process difficult experiences without needing to relive them in conversation.

- ◆ Give survivors a sense of control over their story.

- ◆ Connect people to a community of others who understand their pain.

- ◆ Bring joy, purpose and hope after periods of darkness.

Let's explore different ways creative expression can help in the healing process.

2. Spoken Word and Poetry: Turning Pain into Power

Poetry and spoken word allow people to give voice to their emotions in a way that's both raw and powerful. Words that might be hard to say in conversation flow freely on the page or stage.

A. Spoken Word as an Outlet

Spoken word is more than just poetry. It's a form of story-telling, using rhythm, voice, and emotion to bring words to life. Many survivors of abuse and trauma use it to reclaim their power.

Andre's Story

Andre, 18, grew up in a home where yelling and threats were constant. He bottled up his emotions for years, unsure how to process the pain. That changed when he attended an open mic night at a community center. Inspired, he wrote his first poem about witnessing his parents' fights. Performing it gave him a **sense of control** over his own story, and for the first time, he felt heard.

B. Writing Prompts for Healing

Want to try spoken word or poetry for healing? Here are some prompts:

♦ Write a letter to your past self. What would you tell them?

♦ Describe a place where you feel safe and strong.

♦ If your pain had a voice, what would it say?

3. Music & Songwriting: Turning Emotion into Sound

Music has the ability to heal deep wounds. Whether you write lyrics, compose beats, or just listen to songs that resonate with your emotions, music can be a lifeline.

A. Music as Therapy

Studies show that music can **lower anxiety, improve mood, and reduce stress.** Playing an instrument or writing songs allows people to express emotions in a way that feels natural and freeing.

Jasmine's Story

Jasmine, 17, survived an abusive relationship that left her feeling broken. She had always loved music but never wrote her own songs. After leaving the relationship, she picked up her guitar and wrote about her pain. Writing and singing helped her **find her voice again,** literally and emotionally.

B. Creating a Personal Healing Playlist

Music affects emotions deeply. Create a healing playlist filled with songs that:

♦ Make you feel empowered.

♦ Help you release sadness.

◆ Give you hope for the future.

Some people create transformation playlists… starting with songs that reflect their pain, transitioning to songs of hope, and ending with songs that inspire strength.

4. Visual Arts: Painting, Drawing, & Collage

Art allows people to express things they might not have words for. Sometimes, emotions are too overwhelming to describe, but **colors, textures, and images** can bring them to life.

A. The Science of Art Therapy

Art therapy is often used to help survivors of trauma process their experiences. It's not about creating perfect artwork, it's about expressing emotions in a way that feels safe.

Ways to Use Art for Healing:

◆ Paint an abstract piece using colors that reflect your emotions.

◆ Draw a symbol that represents your personal strength.

◆ Create a vision board with words and images that represent your future goals.

Maya's Story

After experiencing verbal abuse at home, Maya felt invisible. At a youth center, she joined an art program where she painted how she felt inside. The more she painted, the more she realized she wasn't alone. Art became a way for her to **release her pain and build confidence.**

5. Dance & Movement: Healing Through the Body

Trauma often lives in the body. That's why dance, yoga, and movement-based expression can be powerful tools for healing.

A. Why Movement Helps

After experiencing trauma, some people disconnect from their bodies. Dance and movement help release built-up tension and emotions in a healthy way.

B. Ways to Use Dance for Healing

◆ Freestyle dancing: letting emotions guide movement.

◆ Yoga or Stretching: releasing tension stored in the body.

◆ Choreographing a routine based on your story.

Laila's Story

Laila, 16, had always loved dancing, but after experiencing emotional abuse, she lost her passion. One day, she played a song she used to love and let herself move freely. As she danced, she felt strong and connected to herself again.

6. Storytelling and Journaling: Owning Your Narrative

Writing about experiences is a powerful way to process emotions and take back control of your own story.

A. Why Journaling Works

Journaling helps organize thoughts, track healing progress, and release bottled-up emotions.

B. Journal Prompts for Healing

♦ Write about a time you felt strong. What gave you that strength?

♦ Describe a version of yourself who is fully healed. What do they look like? What do they say?

♦ List 5 things you love about yourself.

Malik's Story

Malik, 15, never told anyone about the emotional abuse he faced at home. One day, he started writing letters to his future self, imagining a life where he felt safe and free. Those letters became a roadmap for his healing journey.

7. Finding Your Own Creative Outlet

Not everyone heals in the same way. Maybe spoken word isn't for you, but painting is. Maybe music doesn't resonate with you, but movement does. The key is to find what speaks to your soul.

♦ Try different creative outlets and see what feels right.

♦ Don't focus on skill, focus on expression.

♦ Remember, use creativity as a tool for healing, not perfection.

Conclusion: Your Voice Matters

Healing is a journey, and creative expression is one of the most powerful tools available. Whether through music, dance, poetry or visual art, there is no wrong way to express yourself.

As you move forward, ask yourself:

♦ What form of creativity speaks to me?

♦ How can I use it to process emotions?

- How can I share my story and inspire others?

The next chapter will focus on how to build a strong support system, because healing isn't meant to be done alone.

Reminder: if you or someone you know is struggling, reach out for help. There are people who care about you and resources available.

"The Power of Community"

"No one should stand in the shadows alone,

For love is the seed that our hands have sown.

Brick by brick, we build and rise,

Wiping the tears from weary eyes.

Strength is not in standing apart,

But in the beating of one's great heart.

A hand to hold, and a soul to hear,

Turning sorrow into cheer.

Side by side, we break the chains,

Through every trial and through every pain.

When the world seems cold and small,

Community stands together to embrace all."

Written by: Cassandra L. Williams

CHAPTER 5

THE POWER OF COMMUNITY

You Are Not Alone

Healing is not meant to be done in isolation. Personal growth is important, but true transformation often happens within a supportive community. The people we surround ourselves with such as family, friends, mentors, or advocacy groups can make a difference between feeling stuck and finding the strength to move forward.

This chapter explores how building a strong support system can help survivors of toxic relationships, domestic violence, and emotional abuse heal. It will also provide practical ways to find or create a community that empowers you.

1. Why Community Matters in Healing

Many survivors of abuse or toxic relationships feel alone, ashamed or unheard. Some are afraid to speak up for fear of being judged, while others may not realize that they need help.

But here's the truth:

◆ You deserve to be heard.

◆ You deserve support.

◆ You don't have to heal alone.

Studies show that people who have strong social connections recover from trauma more effectively than those who try to navigate it alone. A healthy support system can:

◆ Remind you that your feelings and experiences are valid.

◆ Offer advice, encouragement and a listening ear.

◆ Help you break free from isolation and self-doubt.

◆ Provide resources and protection when needed.

Let's explore the different types of support systems and how to build them.

2. Finding Your Circle: The Different Types of Support

Not all support looks the same. You may find comfort in friends, family, teachers, coaches or online communities. The key is to identify the people and spaces that uplift and protect you.

A. Trusted Friends

Friends can be powerful allies in healing. A good friend:

◆ Listens without judgment.

◆ Encourages you to set boundaries and stand up for yourself.

- Supports your healing journey, even if they don't fully understand it.

Warning: Not all friends are healthy. If someone minimizes your pain, tells you to "just get over it", or make you feel guilty for talking about your struggles, they may not be a supportive friend.

Kayla and Bri's Story

Kayla had been in an emotionally abusive relationship for a year. When she finally confided in her best friend, Bri, she was nervous about how she would react. But Bri hugged her and said, "I believe you and you deserve better." That moment gave Kayla the strength to start her healing journey.

B. Family Support

For some, family can be a safe and loving source of support. But for others, family may be part of the problem.

- If your family is supportive, let them in. Share your experiences and allow them to help.

- If your family is toxic or dismissive, look for support outside of your home. Your healing is valid, even if your family doesn't understand it.

What if your family doesn't believe you?

It can be heartbreaking when family members dismiss your pain. If this happens, seek support elsewhere such as a counselor, mentor, teacher or advocacy group. You don't have to prove your trauma to anyone.

C. Teachers, Coaches and Mentors

Sometimes, the most unexpected people become our greatest allies. Teachers, coaches, school counselors and mentors can offer guidance and resources when home or social life feels unstable.

If you feel lost, talk to a trusted adult. Many teachers and counselors are trained to help youth dealing with abuse, trauma, and mental health struggles.

Story: Marcus and His Coach

Marcus, 17, grew up in a home where yelling and violence were normal. He never talked about it until his football coach noticed he was struggling. Instead of pressuring him, the coach said, "you don't have to go through this alone." That was the first time Marcus considered asking for help.

D. Support Groups & Community Centers

If you don't feel comfortable talking to friends or family, support groups can be a life-changing resource. Many organizations provide safe spaces for survivors of abuse to share their stories and find healing together.

- ♦ **Local Support Groups:** Community centers, schools or youth programs.

- ♦ **Online Communities:** Social media and mental health platforms offer safe spaces to connect with others.

- ♦ **Creative Groups:** Art, music, or spoken word collectives can provide healing through self-expression.

Safety First: Always make sure online groups are legitimate and safe spaces.

Story: Aaliyah's Healing Circle

After leaving an abusive relationship, Aaliyah, 16, joined a youth poetry group. There she found people who had experienced similar struggles. Through their words and encouragement, she realized she wasn't alone.

3. Setting Boundaries and Protecting Your Energy

A strong community should feel safe, supportive and empowering. But sometimes, well-meaning people can be draining. That's why setting boundaries is an important part of healing.

A. What Healthy Boundaries Look Like

♦ Say no to people who make you uncomfortable.

♦ Taking time for yourself when needed.

♦ Choosing who gets access to your story and emotions.

Red Flag: If someone tries to pressure you into sharing before you're ready, they may not be a safe support system.

4. How to Help a Friend Who's Struggling

Sometimes, you're the one offering support. Here's how to help a friend going through a toxic situation.

♦ **Listen without judgment:** Let them talk without interrupting or questioning their experience.

♦ **Believe them:** Avoid saying, "Are you sure it's that bad" Trust their feelings.

♦ **Encourage professional help:** Share hotlines, counseling resources or support groups.

♦ **Respect their decisions:** Leaving an abusive situation is hard. Be patient.

What Not to Say:

♦ "Why didn't you leave sooner?"

♦ "You're overreacting"

♦ "It's not that bad, other people have it worse"

5. What If You Feel Like You Don't Have a community

If you feel isolated or don't have a strong support system yet, you can build one.

♦ Start by connecting with people who share your values and interests.

♦ Get involved in school clubs, sports or creative groups.

♦ Seek out mentors or online communities that provide sup- port.

Reminder: You deserve to be surrounded by people who make you feel safe, valued, and respected.

Conclusion: You Are Stronger Together

Healing is a journey, and no one should have to walk it alone. Whether it's a trusted friend, mentor or support group, the people around you can help you grow, heal, and find your strength.

Your community is out there. Keep looking until you find it.

Coming up next: Chapter 6, Empowerment Through Education

♦ We'll explore how knowledge is power... learning about your rights, resources, and opportunities to take control of your future.

Reminder: If you need immediate support, reach out to a trusted adult, counselor, or support hotline.

"Rise Through Knowledge"

"They tried to tell me who to be,

To walk in silence and not break free.

But learning lit a spark inside,

a truth too powerful to hide.

Each book I opened the door unlocked,

And each lesson I learned the chains were dropped.

No longer bound by doubt or fear,

The path of wisdom grew so clear.

Know your rights and protect your mind,

And leave the chains of pain behind."

Written By: Cassandra L. Williams

CHAPTER 6

Empowerment Through Education

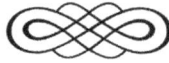

Knowledge is Power

One of the greatest tools for breaking the cycle of abuse and reclaiming your life is education. Not just traditional schooling, but education about **your rights, resources and personal growth.** When you understand what options are available to you, you gain the confidence to make informed decisions about your future. Education is about empowerment. The more knowledge you have, the less power fear and manipulation have over you.

This chapter explores how learning about healthy relationships, personal development, legal rights and career opportunities can help you build a future free from violence and control.

1. Understanding Your Rights

Many people stay in toxic or abusive situations because they don't know their rights. Whether in school, relationships or the legal system, understanding your rights can help you protect yourself and seek help when needed.

A. Your Rights in Relationships

◆ You have the **right** to **say "No"** to anything that makes you uncomfortable.

◆ You have the **right** to **set boundaries** without fear of punishment.

◆ You have the **right** to be **treated with respect**… emotionally, physically and digitally.

◆ You have the **right** to **leave any relationship** that does not serve your well-being.

Warning: If someone tells you that you owe them your time, body or attention, they are violating your rights. Love is built on respect, not control.

B. Your Rights at School

Many students don't realize they have protection against bullying, harassment and discrimination. If you feel unsafe at school because of an abusive relationship or family situation, you have options.

◆ You have the **right** to a **safe learning environment**… schools must protect students from bullying and harassment.

◆ You have the **right** to **counseling and mental health support at most schools.**

◆ You have the **right** to **confidentiality when talking** to school counselors or trusted adults.

◆ If you are in immediate danger at home, you can seek help through school officials who can connect you with protective services.

Action Step: If you feel unsafe at school, speak to a counselor, teacher, or trusted administrator. They are trained to help.

C. Your Rights in the Legal System

Many states have laws that protect minors from domestic violence and dating abuse. These laws can help you get a restraining order, file a police report, or seek protection if you are in danger.

♦ Restraining Orders: Some states allow minors to apply for protective orders against abusive partners or family members.

♦ Confidentiality Laws: Many hot lines and shelters will not share your information with parents or authorities unless you are in immediate danger.

♦ Mandatory Reporting: Teachers, doctors, and counselors are legally required to report abuse if they suspect you are in danger.

If you ever feel unsafe, there are legal protections in place. Reach out to a trusted adult, hotline or counselor for guidance.

2. Using Education to Break the Cycle

Education is more than just school. It's about learning the skills and knowledge that will help you break free from negative patterns and create a brighter future.

A. Developing Life Skills for Independence

Sometimes, survivors of abuse feel trapped because they don't know how to live independently. Learning basic life skills can build confidence and freedom.

♦ Financial Literacy: Learning how to budget, save money, and apply for jobs can help you become financially independent.

- Time Management: Prioritizing school, work, and self-care can keep you focused on long-term success.

- Healthy Decision-making: Understanding how to set goals, avoid toxic situations, and create a plan for your future.

Action Step: Start learning about budgeting, career paths, and healthy habits. These skills can give you tools to build a better life.

B. Exploring Your Career and Education Options

Many young people feel stuck in negative environments because they don't see a way out. But education and career opportunities can be a path to freedom and self-sufficiency.

- **College & Scholarships:** There are many scholarships available for students, overcoming adversity.

- **Trade Schools & Certifications:** If college isn't for you, careers in fields like cosmetology, mechanics or technology can provide financial independence.

- **Entrepreneurship:** Many survivors turn their pain into purpose by starting businesses or advocacy work.

Action Step: Research career paths that excite you and start setting goals.

Story: Lisa's Path to Independence

Lisa grew up in a toxic home environment where she was constantly belittled and controlled. She didn't think she had a future until a teacher encouraged her to apply for scholarships.

With guidance, she earned a full ride to college and is now studying psychology to help others who have experienced trauma.

Lesson: Education opens doors to possibilities you may not even realize exist.

3. Seeking Support & Mentorship

No one succeeds alone. Mentors, teachers, and support groups can help you navigate challenges and find opportunities.

- **Find a Mentor:** A coach, teacher, or older student who has been through similar struggles can offer guidance.

- **Join Support Networks:** Many community organizations help young people build confidence, career skills, and personal development.

- **Ask Questions:** Never be afraid to reach out for advice. There are people who wants you to succeed.

Action Step: Identify at least one mentor or role model you can learn from.

A. Overcoming Fear and Self-Doubt

Many survivors of toxic environments struggle with self-doubt. They think:

These are Lies:

- "I'm not smart enough."

- "People want to see me fail, not succeed."

- "I don't deserve a better life."

Education, in school, trade programs or life experience helps replace those lies with confidence and opportunity.

These are the Truth:

- You are capable of success.

- You deserve a future free from pain.

◆ You are more powerful than your past.

Action Step: Write down one goal you have for your future and one small step you can take toward it.

Story: Malik's Mindset Shift

Malik, 17, didn't believe in himself. His father always told him he'd never amount to anything, and he started to believe it. But when he joined a mentorship program at his local youth center, he realized he had potential. He started working toward a certification in graphic design and now dreams of owning his own business.

"The biggest battle isn't external, it's internal. When you believe in yourself, anything is possible."

Conclusion: Your Future Starts Now

Education, formal or self-taught is the key to breaking cycles, creating independence and reclaiming your life.

◆ Knowledge is power.

◆ Your circumstances do not define your future.

◆ You have the right to seek help, learn and grow.

In the next chapter, we'll explore how to break free from toxic cycles actively, heal generational wounds, and rewrite your story.

Reminder: If you need educational resources, career guidance, or mental health support, reach out to a counselor, mentor or local organization. You are not alone.

"Break The Cycle"

"I found my voice in the depth of my pain.
No longer the prisoner bound by a chain.
No more apologies for taking up space,
No more shrinking and no more disgrace.
I stand in my power, and I speak and fight,
Breaking the cycle and reclaiming my light."
Written By: Cassandra L. Williams

CHAPTER 7

BREAKING THE CYCLE

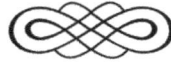

The Power to Change Your Story

Breaking the cycle of violence, abuse, or toxic patterns is not easy, but it is possible. Many people grow up believing that their environment defines them, that they are destined to repeat the same mistakes, or that they are powerless to change their future. **This is not true.**

Cycles, some are toxic such as, abusive relationships, negative thinking or unhealthy habits which they are learned patterns. What is learned can be unlearned. And what is broken can be rebuilt.

This chapter is about taking back control, rewriting your story, and creating a future that is healthier, safer, and filled with self-worth, love and purpose.

1. Understanding the Cycle of Trauma and Abuse

Trauma often repeats itself across generations. Many young people who experience domestic violence, emotional abuse, or neglect grow up and unknowingly enter similar relationships or exhibit the same patterns they once suffered from.

But just because a pattern has existed in your life or family does not mean it has to continue.

A. Recognizing Unhealthy Patterns

Breaking the cycle starts with **awareness**. Ask yourself:

♦ Have I seen toxic relationships modeled in my family or surroundings?

♦ Do I struggle with self-worth or confidence because of past experiences?

♦ Have I entered relationships that mirror what I grew up seeing?

Action Step: Write down one unhealthy pattern you've noticed in your life and commit to changing it.

2. Healing Begins with You

Breaking the cycle is not just about avoiding toxic relationships. It's about healing yourself from past pain, so you don't carry it into your future.

A. Addressing Your Own Trauma

Many people bury their past pain instead of dealing with it. But healing doesn't come from avoidance. It comes from understanding and processing what you've been through.

♦ **Journaling:** Writing about your experiences helps you make sense of your emotions.

♦ **Therapy or Support Groups:** Talking with a trusted counselor or support system can help you work through trauma.

♦ **Self-Reflection:** Asking yourself, "How has my past shaped me? What do I need to unlearn?"

Action Step: Take time to reflect on how past experiences have shaped your thoughts and behaviors. What do you need to heal from?

3. Choosing Healthy Relationships

Once you begin healing, you'll start to recognize what a healthy relationship looks like and what it doesn't.

A. Redefining Love

If you grew up seeing toxic, controlling or abusive relationships, it can be hard to know what a healthy relationship should feel like.

A healthy relationship include:

Respect for each other's feelings and boundaries.

♦ Open and honest communication.

♦ Support without control.

♦ Safety, emotionally and physically.

Warning Signs of an Unhealthy Relationship:

♦ You feel afraid to express yourself.

♦ Your partner or friend tries to control you.

♦ You are constantly blamed for their actions.

♦ You feel drained, anxious or less confident because of them.

Action Step: Make a list of qualities you want in a healthy relationship. Compare them to your current relationships. Do they match?

4. Learning to Set Boundaries

Breaking the cycle, means learning how to say No to toxic behaviors.

What Healthy Boundaries Look Like

♦ Saying No without feeling guilty.

♦ Walking away from relationships that make you feel unsafe.

♦ Knowing that you don't have to explain or justify protecting your peace.

What Happens When You Set Boundaries

Toxic people often don't like boundaries. They might try to guilt-trip you, get angry or make you feel like you're being selfish. Standing up for yourself is never wrong.

Story: Kiara's Boundary Breakthrough

Kiara, 17, grew up watching her mom stay in toxic relationships. When she found herself in one, she was afraid to leave. But after learning about boundaries and self-respect. Kiara told her boyfriend that she wouldn't tolerate his controlling behavior anymore. She left and never looked back.

Action Step: Write down one boundary you need to set in your life and commit to enforcing it.

5. Transforming Pain into Purpose

Some of the strongest people are those who have been through pain and turned it into something meaningful.

A. Using Your Story to Inspire Others

Many survivors of abuse and trauma go on to:

♦ Become advocates and help others escape similar situations.

- Use spoken word, music or art to express their journey.

- Build careers in counseling, education, or activism to create change.

Story: Malik's Mission

Malik, 19, was raised in a violent home and once thought he would never escape the cycle. But after finding mentorship, therapy, and support, he decided to help other young men heal from trauma. Today, he runs a youth organization that teaches boys about healthy masculinity and emotional strength.

Action Step: Think about how you can use your experiences to help others. Could you volunteer? Speak about your story?

Create Art?

6. The Power of Self-Worth

Breaking the cycle isn't just about avoiding toxic relationships. It's about building a life where you truly believe you deserve better.

A. Changing the Way You See Yourself

Many people who grow up in toxic environments struggle with

low self-worth. They believe things like:

- "I don't deserve happiness."

- "I'll never be good enough."

- "No one will love me the way I am."

These are Lies.

Healing means rewriting those beliefs.

- "I am worthy of love and respect."

- "I don't need to prove my worth to anyone."

- "My past does not define my future."

Action Step: Write down three positive affirmations about yourself and say them daily.

7. Creating a Future Free from Toxic Cycles

Breaking the cycle isn't just about escaping toxic relationships. It's about building a new future based on love, respect and self- empowerment.

- Surround yourself with positive, supportive people.

- Invest in your education, career, and personal growth.

- Practice self-care and emotional healing.

- Help others who are stuck in toxic cycles.

Action Step: Create a vision board or write a journal entry describing the life you want to build.

Conclusion: You Are the Change

Breaking the cycle of abuse, trauma, or unhealthy patterns is one of the bravest things you can do.

- You are not your past.

- You are not your mistakes.

- You are not what others have done to you.

"You are the change. You are the future. You are stronger than the cycle."

In the next chapter, we will talk about turning healing into action. How to build a life filled with purpose, passion and peace.

Reminder: If you need support in breaking free from toxic cycles, reach out to a mentor, counselor, or support group. You are never alone.

"Victory Within"

"I once was a story written in pain
Etched in whispers with hope down the drain.
The battle in me raged, both loud and deep
A war I fought when none could see.
Behind the depths of my cries,
I took off my disguise.
No longer trapped in hollow lies.
Learning that strength is more than might.
It's raising up through darkest nights,
Not waiting for the world to see,
But claiming victory inside of me.
No longer bound by fear's embrace
I've gathered strength and found my place."
Written By: Cassandra L. Williams

CHAPTER 8

SHAPING THE FUTURE

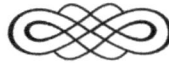

Your Future Begins Now

Healing isn't just about breaking free from the past. It's about building a future that is full of purpose, joy and self-worth. The scars of trauma and unhealthy relationships don't have to define you. They can become the foundation of your strength, proof that you have overcome, survived and are ready to thrive.

Shaping your future means creating a life that reflects your **values, dreams, and personal growth**. It means setting goals, finding meaning, and surrounding yourself with the right people.

In this final chapter, we will explore how to move forward with confidence and create a life that is filled with hope, empowerment, and success.

1. Redefining Your Identity

For many people who have experienced abuse, toxic relation- ships, or trauma, their identity has been shaped by pain. They see themselves through the lens of their past experiences rather than their full potential. But you are more than what happened to you.

A. Who Are You Beyond Your Pain?

Ask yourself:

♦ What do I love to do?

♦ What makes me feel happy and fulfilled?

♦ What kind of person do I want to become?

Action Step: Write down three things that define you outside of your past. They could be your creativity, kindness, strength, or ambitions.

A. Letting Go of Labels

People who have hurt you may have tried to define you, telling you that you're not good enough, not worthy, or not strong enough to succeed. It's time to let go of those labels and embrace a new identity that reflects your true worth.

2. Setting Goals for Your Future

Dreaming for a better future is the first step. Taking some action is what makes it real. Setting small, achievable goals can help you move forward with confidence.

A. The Power of Goal Setting

♦ Helps you stay focused on your personal growth.

♦ Builds confidence by proving to yourself that you can accomplish things.

♦ Creates a vision for a life beyond survival, enabling one filled with joy and success.

B. How to Set Realistic Goals

Follow the **SMART** method:

♦ **S**pecific: What exactly do you want to achieve?

♦ **M**easurable: How will you track progress?

♦ **A**chievable: Is this goal realistic?

♦ **R**elevant: Does this goal align with your future?

♦ **T**ime-bound: Set a deadline to keep yourself accountable.

Action Step: Write down one short-term goal and one long-term goal.

3. Creating a Healthy Environment for Growth

Your surroundings shape your future. The people you interact with, the places you spend time in, and the energy you allow into your life all influence your growth.

A. Choosing the Right People

Surround yourself with people who uplift and inspire you rather than those who drain you or pull you back into unhealthy patterns. Ask Yourself:

♦ Do my friends encourage my personal growth?

♦ Do they respect my boundaries?

♦ Do they celebrate my successes rather than tear me down?

Action Step: Make a list of people in your life who support your healing and growth. If the list feels short, seek out mentors, support groups or new friendships that align with your journey.

B. Finding Your Safe Spaces

Identify places that can bring you peace, this could be a library, community center, art studio, or a quiet park. If home is not a safe place, find support groups, school programs or trusted adults who can provide guidance and security.

Action Step: Find or create a space that allows you to heal and grow. This could be a creative hobby, a new job or a supportive group of friends.

4. Turning Pain into Purpose

One of the most powerful ways to heal is to use your experiences to help others. Many people who have survived trauma, abuse or toxic relationships find meaning in giving back to others.

A. How to Use Your Story for Good

♦ **Advocacy:** Share your experiences to raise awareness about domestic violence, mental health or self-worth.

♦ **Creativity:** Express your journey through spoken word, music or art.

♦ **Mentorship:** Help others who are going through what you've experienced.

Story: Jasmine's Advocacy Journey

Jasmine, 19, grew up in a household filled with emotional abuse. She spent years thinking she was powerless. But after attending a youth empowerment program, she found her voice through spoken word poetry. Today, she performs at schools, inspiring others to speak up and believe in their worth.

Action Step: Think about one way you can turn your past struggles into something positive. It could be joining a support group, creating art or helping a friend in need.

5. Building Emotional Resilience

Life will still have challenges. But resilience means knowing how to handle setbacks without falling back into toxic cycles.

A. Strengthening Your Mental Health

♦ Practice self-care daily, whether it's journaling, music or taking time to rest, an activity of your choice.

♦ Learn coping strategies for stress and triggers.

♦ Seek therapy or counseling if needed because healing is a lifelong journey.

Action Step: Create a self-care routine that helps you feel calm, centered, and strong.

6. Embracing Your Full Potential

You have survived. Now, it's time to thrive.

A. The Future Is Yours to Create

You are not defined by where you come from. You are defined by where you choose to go. So, chase your passions, whether they be writing, business, music, activism or education. Keep growing, learning and challenging yourself. And know that you deserve love, success and happiness.

Conclusion: You Are Unstoppable

Breaking the cycle isn't just about leaving behind toxic patterns. It's about embracing a future filled with purpose, self-worth and confidence.

Your past does not define you.

You are worthy of happiness and success. You have the power to shape your future.

"Your story is still being written, and you are the author." Your Journey Forward

- ◆ Write a letter to your future self, stating what you want to achieve in the next five years?

- ◆ Create a vision board with your dreams, goals and inspirations.

- ◆ Find one way to invest in your future today. It could be anything like, signing up for a class, talking to a mentor or making a commitment to self-care.

Reminder: Healing is not a straight path. There will be setbacks, but every step forward, no matter how small it's a victory.

You are powerful. You are worthy and your future is waiting for you.

This book was written for you, to remind you that no matter what you've been through, you have the power to create a beautiful, meaningful life. Your healing journey is just beginning. Keep moving forward, never stop believing in yourself.

Thank you for taking this journey.

About the Author

Cassandra Williams is a visionary CEO of Reign Global Studios, a premier film production company based in Phoenix, Arizona. With a deep passion for the healing arts and spoken word, she has dedicated her career to creating transformative cinematic experiences that inspire, uplift, and bring about positive change in the world. Under her leadership, Reign Global Studios has become a beacon for storytelling that bridges art and healing, producing films that resonate with authenticity and purpose. Cassandra is a trailblazer in her field. She is committed to using the power of creative expression to heal hearts, amplify voices and spark meaningful conversations globally.

You can connect with me on:

Ⓖ https://linktr.ee/reignstudios411

🅕 https://www.facebook.com/C1assy1